Poor Black Kids
Can Learn Too!

How To Address The Poverty And
Social & Emotional Learning
Challenges Of Black Students

Dr. Jesse W. Jackson III

Plant A Seed Publishing & Media
Rochester, Mi

Acknowledgements:
To a group of all-star Urban Educators & Parents
Mrs. T. Neal, Mr. Larry Johnson, The Student
Support Staff, The Dean of Students Staff And ALL
The Security Team (Grand Rapids, MI)
Mrs. T. Neal & Ms. R. Robinson And Staff (Detroit
Academy of Arts & Science)
Mrs. Beatrice Mayes and Beatrice Mayes Institute
Staff (Houston, Texas)
Mrs. Belinda Raines (Detroit, MI)
Mrs. Ursula Leonard & Ms. Tyus
(Detroit Northwestern, Detroit, MI)
Mr. Jackson & The Woodward Academy Staff
(Detroit, MI)
Mr. T. Russell & Millennium Staff (Columbus, OH)
Dr. Ryan (San Diego, CA)
Mr. L. Johnson (Washington, D.C.)
Dr. Belle (Franklin, VA)
W. Rhodes (Baltimore, MD)

You all are great motivation to me to achieve
excellence. Thank you for giving your lives and
dedicating your work to educating and saving lives
of Black students in America. On behalf of the
thousands of students and parents you have helped
to beat to streets, I want to say thank you.

Published by Plant A Seed Publishing & Media
P.O. Box 80773
Rochester, MI 48308

Printed in the USA

Visit our Websites at www.jessejackson3rd.org and www.plantaseedconsulting.com.

Printed in the USA

ISBN 978-0-9829901-7-9

Library of Congress Control Number: 2013920326

1st Edition: November 2013

Discounts on books are available for bulk purchases.
To order this books for your business, church,
college, or university, please write or call:

Plant A Seed Publishing & Media

P.O. Box 80773

Rochester, MI 48308

1-888-987-5093
Please allow 1-2 weeks for shipping
Order online at: www.plantaseedmedia.com

Table of Contents

Introduction

How does one help the 21st century Title I Black student and parent? Title I is intended to improve academic achievement for disadvantaged populations. A closer look at how the title code is broken down clearly shows that Title I funds were put in place to help those who are economically disadvantaged. To be effective in helping young people who are being raised in poverty, we have to change our strategy. This book is aimed at helping Title I providers and educators to identify with the populations they serve and understand some new innovative methods that need to be in place to make a difference.

To qualify for Title I services, a family's income must fall within the guidelines for free or reduced lunch at school. One key characteristic I want to look at is the social aspect of poverty. I want to explore the social influences and characteristics of our students so we can be aggressive in addressing the issues and providing the services to help young people avoid being economically disadvantaged. It has been said that knowledge is power. However, the truth is that knowledge is power only if it's accepted and used properly. Therefore, we as educators have to step up our game.

Too many educators feel sorry for this group, and sympathy makes it impossible to effectively teach someone. Sympathy disables a teacher's ability to confront and challenge the student. On the other hand, empathy helps teachers understand, but does not allow students to make excuses and pull punches. Students and parents raised in poverty have to be given the truth so they can grow.

Unfortunately, we have a generation of teachers who are afraid to confront this group of students and parents because of fear – fear of the response, fear of hurting their feelings or fear of being called a racist. Many also lack the ability to communicate with impoverished children, so they don't confront and they don't challenge. This trend has set low expectations for the students and poor effort by educators. Laziness has become the brand on modern public inner-city schools. Many educators do just enough to get by, only what their contract calls for. Many have basically given up on this group of students, leading them to a life of certain mediocrity or failure. This attitude is unacceptable. It would be unfair to say all educators fall into this category. There are an abundance of all-star educators who give 120 percent toward helping this population and meet every challenge presented, like Joyce McDowell in Smithfield, VA; Ashauna Short and Dennice R. Robertson, Guilford County Schools in Greensboro, NC; Mrs. Neal & Larry Johnson in Grand Rapids, MI, Mrs. T. Neal & Ms. R. Robinson And Staff in Detroit, MI and Beatrice Mayes in Houston, TX, to name a few. These educators have given their lives to serving the Black community. If any of these great people work for your district, it would be wise to keep and pay them whatever they ask to be paid, because they are valuable.

Additionally, the challenges of working with this population have burned out many teachers. They have given 100 percent and have reached the point of mental fatigue. Many have been caught ill prepared to manage these changes and challenges of working with Black students and parents. We have taken 20 years off in our course of innovation and have been left behind. We have gotten tired. What I want is to provide awesome new strategies that will help teachers, principals, and service coordinators to work with students and parents in the most efficient and productive way.

"It is the supreme art of the teacher to awaken joy in creative expression and knowledge."

- Albert Einstein -

Chapter 1
Changes In The Population

One of the major demographics in working with Black students is family structure. The population has changed the system of education forever. The current school system was not designed or developed to meet the needs of the 21st century Black students and parents. It was built on prior ideas and for a prior population that typically came from two-parent homes, and homes not classified as poor.

This is why there was such opposition back in the mid-60s to making a national curriculum. The issue is that the playing field is not the same. It has been commonly known that whoever has the gold will typically win the fight. The creation of the Title I bill was evidence that the government acknowledged that social factors are extremely crucial in academic achievement. Consider these facts (from the U.S. Census Bureau):

- Over 25 million children live apart from their biological fathers (that is 1 out of every 3 children in America, or 33.3 percent).
- 6.1 million children younger than 18 live with their grandparents.
- 14 million single parents in the United States are responsible for raising 21.2 million children (approximately 26 percent of children under 21 in the United States today).
- The nation's prisons held approximately 744,200 fathers and 65,600 mothers in 2007.

- Parents held in the nation's prisons reported having an estimated 1,706,600 minor children, accounting for 2.3 percent of the U.S. resident population under age 18.
- 48% of the nation's 50 million public school students are low income. (Southern Education Foundation)
- 1 in 4 children lives in a household that struggles to put food on the table. That's 16.7 million children.
- 10% of children and adolescents suffer from a mental illness that is severe enough to cause some level of impairment.
- Black male unemployment is highest, at 12.7 percent (www.dol.gov)

These demographics alone change the emotional makeup of the classroom. These statistics have had a great impact on our education system, and we have been ill-equipped to manage it. We have been bombarded with these demographic changes in our students for 20 years, but we have not changed. While there was an emphasis on having No Child Left Behind, professionals and the leadership got left behind. We got caught looking at the things that are of minor importance and neglected the most important things such as the needs of our customers, students, parents and colleagues. One major negative of the No Child Left Behind Act was that it created a theory of accountability.

There is no problem with being accountable, but a lot of people were ill-prepared for that, because they took the failing of the students personally. Unfortunately, this played on the insecurities of some and has created great division. Parents are against teachers; teachers are against parents. Principals are against teachers, and parents are against principals. This negative disposition has caused us to look for someone to blame rather than looking at the root causes of the student failure. This has created an individualistic environment. Education is a team and love sport. You love what you do and love who you serve – students and parents. This is the only way we can help Black students and parents to be successful in their education and life.

This book will teach you how to challenge the poverty mindset of our students and parents. Poverty has to be confronted and challenged or it will become over powering. Why? Because a person who has nothing is accustomed to taking, whether it is emotionally or physically. This is why so many teachers and principals are drained at the end of each school day, because the clients take all day. This is why we are going to need to be much smarter in how we work with Black students and parents.

Social Poverty

America's number one indicator of poverty is whether you are born out of wedlock and live separated from your father. That's a powerful truth and it does not get addressed. It's not an indictment of the mother. It is an indictment purely of the father. A lot of times mothers are being dumped and left with all of these issues, and the father walks away and leaves the bill. He's leaving financial oppression.

"Your role as a leader is even more important than you might imagine. You have the power to help people become winners."

--Ken Blanchard

Chapter 2
Why Welfare Has Ruined America

One of welfare's major destructive kick-backs came when Aid to Dependent Children (ADC) was put into place. ADC dictated that fathers could not be present in the home if the family was to receive aid. That caused many minorities (black and Hispanic, low-income white men) to feel like less than men. Because they had low resources, a lot of guys were not interested in being fathers. This is no excuse; it just identifies true feelings of men throughout this country. Millions of men have been abandoned by their fathers and were never taught how to prosper and be successful in life. Those types of policies attached to receiving aid made men who already felt badly about not being able to take care of their families feel worse. This contributed to decreasing fathers' involvement in the lives of their children and promoted an unhealthy relationship between impoverished men and women.

Today, many impoverished people use having children as an economic strategy to financially take care of themselves. They have a child to get and stay on government assistance. The government will take care of housing and food, and will give them a monthly stipend. This is a dangerous mentality, a dangerous truth.

The education system has been damaged by the decomposition of these social factors. This simply means the home has fallen apart. Our home structure has been weakened, and welfare has been at the center of that.

Poor Kids Can Learn TOO!

The government has spent $13 trillion over the past 30 years to aid the poor and has created an incentive for people to remain poor because they know they will get help. A person who is content with poverty is satisfied with $500 a month. As a professional educator, you can't look at that and say, "Well it's just a little money." Listen, a poverty mind is a scarcity mind. A scarcity mind will take what it can get. If they're not working for it, they feel like they are winning and all of us who go to work every day are fools. That's what the poverty/welfare mind has created. It has enabled people not to work and receive something for doing nothing. It's made people be deceitful and find ways to manipulate the system.

Welfare has financially crippled people with the mentality of making "just enough to get by." It has also created the entitlement mentality. As a matter of fact, most human services benefits are called entitlements. Entitlement means you are owed something. This is an atrocious message to send because the system does not owe them anything. It's a dangerous mentality. It's one thing to help the poor and impoverished, but it's another thing to enable people to manipulate and take advantage of the system. So we, as professionals, have to understand what we're dealing with and overcome it.

Hidden Effects

Working with economically disadvantaged students and parents has had a negative effect on the professional staff. Many social workers and Title I educators have been disheartened by the frequent misuse and abuse of benefits that many parents receive. It is insulting when a hard-working person who struggles to make ends meet sees people who don't work every day receive money, free food and housing assistance by manipulating the system. The spirits of social workers and educators have been broken and morale is low because professionals are not seeing the results they want. We got into the helping profession because we wanted to see people's lives change, and we're not seeing that happen. This is the type of thing you've got to watch out for as a teacher. A lot of times, you're giving your heart and soul and you're not seeing the results you want, and that can be very depressing.

The welfare system has literally contributed to AWOL fathers who know their children can get benefits or food assistance, and will be OK. Many men are not MAN-ing UP. They are not being responsible for their children, and this has created one of the most dangerous epidemics of all time.

Speaking as a black person,
welfare is the worst thing
that's ever happened to us.
--Charles Evers

Chapter 3
The Birth of The Poverty Mind
How Poverty Affects Our Students

Many social factors are involved in the damage of the Black parent and student mind – what I call the poverty mind. The poverty mind is always looking for a shortcut. The poverty mind is always looking for somebody to make things easy for them, or give them a handout. Those with the poverty mind have an inferiority complex, low self-esteem and are very sensitive.

In many places where you have low self-esteem, the rates of violence are high, as are the rates of anger management and delinquent behavior among youths and parents. Parents with an inferiority complex tend to become negatively engaged in their child's education. Coming to the school to confront and be negative toward teachers and principals is a dangerous practice because it does not contribute to the overall outcome that we are looking for in our schools. It's actually counterproductive and disappointing.

This also contributes to serious academic failure in two ways. First, the students may not understand or know the work and teachers have been trained to teach a certain way, while 21st century students with a poverty mind are geared toward learning in a nontraditional manner. The poverty mind is geared toward instant gratification. We all went to college for multiple years. We were trained to sit and listen to the professor or fail. A two-hour lecture is normal for most of us. However, the 21st century poverty mind is not equipped for that. We were all trained in traditional education. We were not trained to work with Black students and parents, the economically disadvantaged. This requires a different skill set and mind frame, and this is what we hope will come out of this book.

There are several major factors to consider when educating the economically disadvantaged youth.

1. Negative images of themselves.

Most economically disadvantaged people have negative images of themselves mirrored by their poverty. Unfortunately, the average impoverished black youth identifies him or herself with the street life – with being pimps, whores, booty shakers, rappers, tough guys, or gang members. These negative images breed negative conduct. Young poor black boys refer to themselves as pimps or gangsters, and boys get involved in gangs because they have a negative image of themselves.

2. Generational history.

For many of our students and parents, this is the third time they've been involved in a Title I school, getting free or reduced lunch. Schools start fighting the generational cycle of family poverty and failure, and the goal should be to transition students and parents off a low-economic status. If a family is still disadvantaged at the end of the program, it didn't work. If you have a program for improving disadvantaged people, they should not be disadvantaged at the end of it. That's not hard to understand. Of course, an intellectual can try to confuse everybody and say, "That's not necessarily true." Well, you're not focused on outcome. We have to look for outcomes that can be measured economically, not in test scores and letter grades.

3. Prison enrollment and incarceration.

As we said before, 800,000-plus incarcerated parents are responsible for more than 1,700,000 youth. Those kids are suffering because they automatically qualify for Title I services, free or reduced lunch, in most cases. Then, you're dealing with the social aspect of what kind of mental picture the young person is enduring trying to manage a Title I frame of mind. You have to be able to help the students manage all these factors.

These are the factors that make the difference in our ability to understand our students and their needs. This book is about addressing the social factors. We're not dealing with the academic challenges quite yet. The social factors play a major part and influence the academic factors.

Education is the key to unlock
the golden door of freedom.
-George Washington Carver

Chapter 4
Schools Vs The Streets

The streets are our greatest competition in Black Title I schools. Millions of impoverish students have fallen victim to the misleading appearance of streets. The streets are a predator for young black boys and females. The streets mislead black boys into believing that school is for dummies. The streets mislead young black females into believing that having a guy baby will solidify a relationship. The streets have stolen millions of students and parents dreams via violence, teen pregnancy, substance abuse, depression and incarceration. The influence of the streets, which has been defined as the fast life is completely deceiving. Life is a long term game. The streets represent shortcuts and a short life. Black Title I schools have not been able to compete with the streets because it refuses to come off its high horse. The streets are dominating the urban areas because our Black Title I Schools are ill equipped to fight this war.

The first issue is schools lack the understanding of the opponent, "the streets". The truth is that the streets are a product of father and family failure. The streets offers the daddy substitute, fake love, hands on learning, quick cash, entrepreneurship, protection, fun and excitement. Our Black Title I schools have offered us mean teachers, uncaring staff, handouts for learning, no financial education, the job mentality, adversarial environments, metal detectors, security and mini police stations in the school. While many of these measures may be necessary, they are unattractive and very poor sales points for a Black student and parent. This why thousands of Black students and parents have left public schools and flocked to charter schools trying to beat the streets. Please consider these differences between many of our schools and our greatest competition, the streets:

- Streets promote the king in black boys (leadership skills).
- The streets impose its values.
- Though illegal, the streets promote entrepreneurial endeavors.
- The streets offer hands on learning.
- The streets is real-time (I need it, I take it). The term fast money has defined the streets. The streets fully disrespects life process of progress. Life says I invest, I let it grow and then I harvest.

- Students must be offered an abundance of experiences (cultural).
- Schools are scare to represent truth.
- Students must be introduced to economic opportunities (entrepreneurial opportunities and knowledge).
- School must be fun and engaging.
- Schools must be real time. Though school is a 12 year, process, we must find a way to provide profitable results for our students during the course of the education process. (current)

In order for a Black Title I school to consistently beat the streets and win our students, we must engage in an urban model of education, which fully acknowledge our differences from mainstream education and provides options for student success.

Poor Kids Can Learn TOO!

Chapter 5
How To Build A 21st Century
Black Title I School

Breaking away from the one size fits all education model is critical in helping us understand the fundamental differences in what is required to teach, educate and be successful in an inner-city Title I school district. My research and abundance of experience has lead me to understand that there are 12 major principles for providing a high quality educational experience in Title I schools. I call these 12 principles "The Urban Model Of Education". This model describes mandatory requirements and basic changes in philosophy will allow urban/ Title I based schools to be better prepared to serve the needs of students, parents, teachers and staff.

1. Urban/ Title I education saves lives.

For kids in an impoverished inner-city community, education has a much different meaning than to kids in the suburbs or in rural areas. Kids in the inner city don't have many outs, directions or options. Education for many of these families is a life-saving mechanism.

This is why we must engage in a fully student-centered mission to address the needs of our population. If we know that education means so much to these kids' lives and that our young people do not have the tools they need to succeed, we must take the extra steps to help. Putting a strong school together is something you can do to help; this is under your umbrella of influence as an educator.

We're losing in the game of education because many urban Title I schools are set up to fit the needs of the professionals, not the students. Continuing to run a school that does not meet the needs of your clients makes you a part of the problem.

2. Urban Title I schools must produce taxpayers, not tax takers.

Right now, urban education and many Title I schools are producing more welfare recipients than in the history of the United States. We have a weak model of education, a weak model of goal setting, a weak model of aspiration seeking. We are producing students with low paradigms of life who see the benefit of being a tax taker. Some believe this is the way to live. As educators, our social mission is to teach and make our students taxpayers via entrepreneurship and good employment. We don't need more minimum wage taxpayers. We need taxpayers who make an economic difference in the lives of their community.

Recessions mean people aren't working. The tax base is dilapidated. We need to produce taxpayers. We can't afford to have drop-out or prison production factories in cities around America. Those places contribute to the recession because these full communities are receiving money from the government but not returning any of it.

In a good district, maybe $10,000 a year will be spent on a kid getting an education. The juvenile system spends up to $118,000 a year on one kid, to lock them up. The investment we're putting in kids' education isn't comparable. This poor investment produces minimum wage job skills. What we need are high-wage earners. When our kids are introduced to high income level jobs and career paths, they go in that direction and the economy grows. The bar is set too low and does not help kids and parents go to a new level. These low expectations and ideas are not helping kids to decide that they want to be something other than a recipient of free food and low-cost housing.

We have to remove this burden on the economy and replace it with a taxpayer ideology. When urban areas don't do well, America's economy will stay in a recession because they suck the money out of the human services, corrections and other systems. The economy works well when people are working, taking care of themselves and buying their own food and medication. The government does not do a good job of taking care of people or educating kids, and really, that's not what the government is for; it's a legislative body that must legislate, not make education policies.

3. Urban Title I schools curriculum must promote post-secondary education.

Post-secondary education essentially states that all kids must graduate and move on to another level. A high school diploma is not enough. President Barack Obama said to us, in one of his initial speeches in February 2009, that dropping out of school is no longer an option. All students in

America must realize that a high school diploma is no longer enough. Everyone needs expanded, extended education to have an opportunity to expand their income. Post-secondary education can mean community college, a university, the military, a skilled trade, business school, vocational trades and specialized skills. Post secondary education is broad. **The kids in the urban areas are not receiving all the available options.**

I remember flying to Virginia and sitting next to an engineering consultant. This lady was in charge of building new energy, green energy, and radioactive nuclear plants. If a new plant was getting built, she was involved in it. We started talking, and she told me that the biggest problem in the field is not having employees – the laborers and skilled tradesmen who can do the jobs in building nuclear, new energy power plant. She also said that many that many of her employees, when they come out of school with the training and education in the skilled trade are making $45,000 and up in their trade. She said that skilled trades such as carpentry, electricity, masonry, boiler operators and more are not repopulating. It's becoming a dying field, thus America's infrastructure is dying out. The African American is not a part of the construction of the country because it requires a certain education, and we have more black men in the juvenile system than in a steel trades programs for electric, electrical construction, masonry, pouring concrete, etc.

This is a problem that must be addressed. This is dangerous, and it is not productive or conducive to a healthy economic outcome. Title I schools must present all of the options to the young people: entrepreneurship, skill trades, community college, the military, medical assistant, medical school, law school – all of these choices have to be presented. The full scale of options must be introduced in our curriculum and in extracurricular programs. It has to be part of our ideas from start to finish, from K through 12. What do you want to be? You can do it. College has to be introduced in preschool.

My daughter is 4 years old and is already running around saying, "I'm going to college." It started after she watched Toy Story 3, and Andy, the kid, is going off to college. We say to her, "Kalynn, are you going to college?" and she responds, "Yes I'm going to college. I am going to Ohio State." She thinks school is fun. It's just the culture of our house.

Our young people are not being prepared for college. That's why they go and flunk out the first year. They're not academically prepared, and they're not socially prepared. This is the job of the educator, to Get Students College Ready! College ready includes all postsecondary options. It's not what we've been taught, but we must do a better job of helping our young people understand their options and preparing them for the future.

4. Urban Title I schools must establish safety and security.

Many times in urban school districts, one of our biggest concerns is that safety and security have been breached. Violence and gang activity are rampant in our schools, and the number one reason people leave school is because they don't feel safe. We've got to do a better job of helping our students and our parents feel safe while on campus.

This means educators have to get more strategic about it. You have to be more aggressive and be on the ground. Some schools that have problems with violence just wait and let things happen. Some schools aggressively interject and get in there with kids, monitoring the situations and helping to diffuse many problems before they start.

One of my superintendent colleagues told me about a building administrator who was afraid of conflict. There was a big brawl at her middle school, and she reviewed it with the superintendent. The building administrator said she had a feeling something was going to happen. My colleague asked the principal why she didn't do anything, and the principal said she didn't know how to do anything.

Safety and security are even more widespread issues in the 21st century age of Facebook. Educators have to understand the gangs in your community and break up that gang activity. You can't just say it's not tolerated. You have to understand what's going on before you can set boundaries. It's going to take more intervention. It's going to take more wisdom in how you do it. Safety and security is number one.

It is about procedure and having the right people who understand what true safety and security mean. You have to understand that you can defuse most problems by just being in the right place at the right time. Many times in the juvenile jail that I worked in, security kept a lot of violent conduct down by just having relationships with the kids. That's being able to understand your environment and the people in it and being able to communicate with the kids and parents to avoid having a hostile relationship. This improves and keeps violence down. **When you see violence and homicide that means you have poor communication.** True safety and security come with awareness, understanding the parameters of the building, communicating with your people and just being hip to what's going on. If you know the cafeteria's a high conflict area, you need strategies in place to make sure that's not an issue. You need people on your team who can manage it.

We need to communicate and talk to kids about how to be peaceable, how to think and how to keep yourselves out of the situation. In my book *"Prison Is Not An Option!"*, I teach 15 life saving actions for black boys. It's these kinds of things we have to teach kids. As administrators and teachers, we have to do more than say "no tolerance" or "drug-free zone." You need people out there monitoring. At many urban school, people smoke marijuana outside or in the bathroom. You might be understaffed, but you need to position people in problem areas and be wiser. You have total control and autonomy over the situation, but you have to be smarter and use your people better. You need some men and women who are not afraid of these young people. If you're afraid, you will lose. You can't be scary, either. You have to be professional, but firm.

Make strong rules and enforce the rules consistently.

You also have to monitor sexual conduct in the school. One statistic I saw one school building said that the highest number of pregnancies were the result of kids having sex in the buildings. That's means people aren't watching. You have to be aggressive, and having cameras in the school is not enough. You have to stop being neglectful and stop being scared to walk the floor. You have to go outside, among your kids, and be sincere about the task. That's the only way you can keep kids, parents and your staff safe. Title I schools must guarantee the safety of staff, students and parent while on school property.

5. Urban Title I schools must have motivated, strong leaders with superior ethics, honesty and integrity.

For far too long, Title I schools have had a problem with our educators stealing and lying. Billions of dollars have been stolen by paying people who don't work or hiring people who are not qualified. Money has been appropriated for kickbacks. This kind of conduct makes everyone question whether a leader can be trusted. This is a cancer to a school system and it makes parents and students wonder which crime is worse. Many urban districts have the attitude that if he stole, then so I can – they're stealing money so I can steal paper; they're stealing computers, so I can steal pencils. It's this kind of attitude that has created the most cancerous, debilitating, awful environments and has caused thousands of urban districts to close thousands of schools. This behavior creates an environment in which you might have a legitimate vendor who can't get in the district because there's so much corruption, so many people stealing, and so many bad deal kickbacks going on.

I know there are many districts like that, that are giving away millions of dollars to friends and buddies. I don't have a problem with hiring friends, as long as the friends are qualified and can deliver the goods. I have a problem with family members get contracts and then not producing the work. Yet they still get paid. And who suffers? Our students. This kind of conduct, by school boards, leaders, principal, assistant principal, teachers, have caused great economic hardships in urban areas.

Stealing from the people you serve is detestable and unethical, and you better check yourself as a person. We took an oath as educators to do certain things and to not do certain things. We took oaths as counselors and social workers to stand for ethics and what's right all the time, not when it is convenient for us. A colleague of mine was a chef for a school district. He said the employees would steal toilet tissue, food, and oil and grease for cooking, and they wonder why districts go into bankruptcy and closing schools. It is because these attitudes: "It's about me and I've got to get mine."

It's always been said that if you give a poor man a budget, he will not spend it, eat it up or steal it. That's because poverty is a mindset; it is how people feel, think and view themselves. We have to understand that poverty has to be attacked. That's

Poor Kids Can Learn TOO!

why I talk to professional staff, building staff and kids about money and about their ideas about wealth and the world. And this is what has to happen in Title I schools in urban areas. Poverty, the spirit, ideas, and mind frame, have got to be attacked. A person can have millions of dollars but still have a poverty mind, and that's when he or she starts stealing money. It's a fear based idea that, "I don't have enough that I've got to take a short cut to get mine." It's poverty.

One of the crimes that your reputation never heals from is being a thief. I challenge you as a leader of an urban Title I school district to model the conduct of what you want your kids to be. **It is unethical for school leaders and teachers to use the union to underperform and keep a job. This causes kids to be set back and their lives to be ruined because you don't want to do the job that you took an oath and you take a paycheck to do. I'm asking you to consider how you live and why you do what you do. Our students cannot afford for you to keep doing it.**

To steal, to misappropriate, to write checks off the school books for your personal use, to pay your house notes with the school funds – this is the epitome of poverty and unethical conduct. It should be prosecuted to the highest extent of the law, and you should live in shame for the rest of your life.

Ethics is what we live by. Leadership ethics is what we must make our life, be invested in because that is all we have. If we breach ethics, we do not have a school system. Morals and values are about ethics. It is not about opinion; it is not about making a mistake. A mistake is something you didn't mean to do. Stealing is an intentional act. It was wrong and you were caught. You need to evaluate why we do what we do, and when you take the lead as a school board member all hate, domestic theories and impoverished thinking must be abolished. **You do not hire people – school board members, principals or building managers – who do not have a solid ethics and honesty.**

If you can't be trusted, you can't be a teacher or educator.

Everybody's appalled when teachers violate ethics codes by engaging in inappropriate relationships with their students, because educators are held to a higher standard. They're like our preachers and police officers. Some of us took a higher call in life. When you became an educator you said you would stand out above the crop in life. When you become a jurist or judge, you're not like everybody else. Unfortunately, we cannot have bad days because we could ruin somebody's life forever. A teacher could crush somebody's self-esteem, and our students' self-esteem is fragile already.

You have to understand that the leadership call of the 21st century is the model of ethics. All I have is my word. And there are a lot of things you can say about Dr. J.W. Jackson III, but you will never be able to call me a thief or a liar. I have a lot of flaws. I have a lot of issues. I make a lot of mistakes – well, maybe not that many – but lying and stealing will not be named among them. My word is my bond. If I tell you I'm going to do something, I follow through. That is the leadership ethics we must have, that promotes a healthy school environment and a healthy reputation throughout the world.

6. Urban Title I school board members and superintendents have to work together.

If you see any urban or public school district where the school board and the superintendent do not get along, I can guarantee you that they will fail. Division is the seed of failure in the education system. When you have school board members making life hard for the superintendent that they hired, it's hard for the person to do the job you brought him or her there to do. Division among leadership is unacceptable. We can disagree, but unity and ability to work together is mandatory if you're going to be successful.

You're going to have to ask yourself some important questions. Can we work together? Can we agree on the budget? Do we have the same vision for the school district? Is the relationship between this board and its superintendent profitable? Are our decisions about students and parents? Do we have a power and control issues? Are we fighting over who has more authority versus the outcome for our parents and students?

These are questions we have to answer. Leadership at the top cannot fight, for any reason. Leadership must display the ultimate unity and respect for one another for the overall outcome of the organization. When you have an organization that is unwilling to work together, and you have a power and control issue at the top – the school board fighting the superintendent on what needs to be done – you've got a dangerous environment. That division trickles down to the staff, and it trickles down to the kids and parents. This has caused a domino effect of unproductive relationships.

The board must work with its board chairs, supervisors and managers for successful outcomes. Supportive and successful relationships are the seed for a successful urban/ Title I school system. If you are having problems in this area, don't hesitate to call us. We specialize in leadership and teamwork development in crisis situations. Locate us at www.plantaseedconsulting.com.

7. Urban Title I school districts must address the issues of race.

If you live or serve students in urban areas, you have to make a more conscious effort to understand the social dynamics of race on education, since these areas typically are poor and have high black and Hispanic populations. The biggest problem in education today is that we have continued to neglect issues of race and culture. Culturally, we are all different, and race influences culture. The education system lacks respect for culture. In places with high Arabic or Hispanic populations, services are provided for those ethnic groups. Why? Because of the language barrier. No education system will allow language to affect the education of a child. **However, when it comes to poor black kids, recognizing the language and cultural differences gets neglected.** It becomes an after-thought.

It is thought that black kids can be treated and taught like any other kid. The African-American culture, as well as the culture of growing up in an urban area, is neglected. The majority of urban city black kids go through family decompensation, fathers leaving home, parents who are emotionally unstable to raise children, mothers who are under stress and buckling in the child-rearing process, and high counts of poverty. The data tell us that more than 16 million kids come to school hungry, and we know, that many of those kids are African-American students. The entire Title I agenda and initiative was to meet the needs of impoverished and economically disadvantaged students. We know that was predominantly black children.

However, we have refused to accept that culturally. The abundance of weak professional development, vacation-based education conferences neglect to address the real issues of urban cities. Language wise, black impoverished kids speak a different language and should not be treated the same as other kids who don't speak the English language. Black culture is dominated by language barriers. Black kids have a different dialect, which includes emotional communication, slang, broken English and violent conduct. However, mainstream society does not understand or respect it or make an attempt to bridge the language barriers.

Slang is destructive and difficult to understand. Slang emerged because of a lack of education and a lack of a respect for education in the black community. **Poor word usage and slang**

talk is a major reason for poverty in this country. Money has a language. When black children don't learn how to communicate in the standard American dialect, they get left behind. Society has allowed some forms of slang to become profitable via hip hop music; however, aside from that, slang and broken English are economic curses that promote poverty. **This is why it is not wise to have an all white (middle class) teaching staff teaching in a predominantly black school.** The problem is not in teaching expertise; the culture and communication gaps gets exposed with issues of classroom management, in school discipline and interaction with the parents. This is where cultural differences truly become relevant.

We all know that our ability to be socialized influences our ability to learn. People who can't speak our language or understand our background will struggle in teaching us. They don't understand the social and emotional factors involved in a child's ability to learn. This is especially true in the areas of black impoverished children. It is apparent that black school districts are judged by double standards, there is great resentment when these issues come to light because many believe in the one-size-fits-all model, and that everybody can learn the same way on the same day at the same level. They try to omit culture and race from deciding the appropriateness of educational services. **This is neglect of the worst kind and has caused many to feel left out or threatened.**

The urban education model does not say that if you're white, you can't teach black kids, or vice

Poor Kids Can Learn TOO!

versa. <u>Instead, it says you have to be highly culturally competent, diverse and sensitive to the socio-economic factors of a person's life.</u> People from impoverished urban districts have been raised in a different culture than people from middle class backgrounds. Culture and the class system are where we see gaps. There are significant differences between the poor and the rich, between middle class and the poor, between the working class and the working poor. **The class system continues to be broken down, but we don't adjust.** We just take our ideas, our preconceived notions, and decide what should happen. People from middle class backgrounds make assessments on what a single mother of 5, 6 or 7 kids who makes $500 a month from a government payment and gets section 8 housing may and may not do for her children.

Those types of social lapses in judgment are unacceptable, and it is not just white people doing it to black people. **Some black people are from a different culture and class system and don't understand what it's like to be brought up in a single-parent home.** They don't know what it's like to be brought up in a class system with no love. That's where the gap of class and culture really place stress on the education system. True diversity training of the highest level is required to be effective as a 21st century Title I educator in the urban education model. We have to understand that we have different social values that separate us. Some people don't believe that to take things from other people without permission is stealing, or they

Poor Kids Can Learn TOO!

believe it's not stealing if they see someone else stealing. That is a gap in social values.

Our education system has numerous social gaps – our ability to communicate, how we interact with one another, what we believe is right or wrong. I had an experience with a charter school I worked with in Detroit. Every teacher was white, and the student body was 99 percent black. As I studied this institution – I worked there for approximately 3 months in a consulting capacity, working with students and observing teachers – I noticed that the social demographics of the kids were not readily understood by the teachers. Most of the teachers came from middle class backgrounds, some even affluent backgrounds. They came to the charter school to teach because they felt comfortable and safe in the structure. Charter schools and their systems and rules can protect these gaps that aren't otherwise protected in public schools, such as weak classroom management, poor oversight of the class, the inability to communicate with parents and students. In public education, the Title 1 legislation mandates that you work with parents, and that parents be involved in the process. In charter schools, the mandates are there, but they are not held to stringent federal oversight.

The issue is that charter schools are set up to put public schools out of business. The restrictions are more relaxed and there is no Union. I was invited to a charter school Dayton, Ohio, by a black school administrator. Her concern was she had a 90 percent white staff and 100 percent black student body. She said that frequently, the white teachers, though they were very caring, admitted that they were socially disconnected from the students this very impoverished part of Dayton, Ohio. They had major problems with communication and it hurt the overall classroom performance of students. There were frequent teacher assaults – kids hitting teachers, throwing chairs, turning over tables – and they didn't know how to manage it. If you take that to a standard union public education classroom, someone from a different social background or who is used to dealing with people from impoverished social backgrounds might be available to help. The thought of kids putting their hands on a teacher is not even socially acceptable. Many teachers who understand population may say things like, "If you put your hands on me, you are going to get dealt with and I'm going to lose my job." As I observed this pathetic education setting with no classroom presence, I watched a student strike a teacher and the teacher just kind of act like it did not happen. The teacher told the student to calm down and be good. That's not proper classroom management, and this highlights great gaps in culture. This type of conduct can happen anywhere, but it is handled differently by different cultures. I know white educators who are very sensitive to how to work with African American students and parents, not fully asserting themselves or speaking the truth because of fear of perception and conflict. **The fact is that any student who is disruptive in the classroom is a cancer to the educational process.** These kids must be managed differently, and not in a traditional classroom. Classroom management and control are not about race, it's about culture. Culture denotes the comfort and ability to communicate.

Many times when I have been in classrooms with a white teacher and black students, the classroom management is hideous. **I've seen it in classrooms with black teachers, as well.** The key factor typically is social class. In many urban areas, a low priority is placed on education. If you cannot comprehend such a low value, then your values will be tested in this system. A lot of educators don't have a command of the classroom. They don't have presence in the classroom or control of the environment, and they don't produce good results. This is why addressing issues of race, culture and socialization in the urban setting is critical in helping Title I educators to maintain control in an urban classrooms.

8. Urban Title I schools must teach advanced social education skills to our students.
In urban areas, many kids come from homes where the traditional parental influences are not there. Typically, we are dealing with single-parent homes or kids living with their grandparents. Kids come from situations that are not traditional and that have no social education.

Fathers are supposed to teach you how to be a gentleman or to respect women, but in these homes, he's not there or doesn't do it as well, and those poor habits come to the school. The decomposition of the family has resulted in the deterioration of "home training" i.e. social skills.

The 21st century Title I urban education system now must address social skills. It is time to invest in our young people with the social skills needed to be productive in life. Many youth need to learn how to communicate, how to live in America and how to get jobs. I remember doing training for the Job Corps organization. The staff told me that it was their job to get young people placed in employment. They could get the kids good paying jobs, but many of these kids couldn't keep the job. They couldn't sell themselves. Over the phone, the counselor could sell the kid. But one on one, the kid didn't have interviewing skills, they didn't know how to socialize themselves, they didn't know how to talk to people, they didn't know how to come to work on time, they didn't know why they couldn't get and keep the job. It was because they were socially ill prepared for the task at hand.

A good friend of mine was a school superintendent. She had a kid she was about to expel. She gave him a book of mine to read about being a good employee. After he read the book, the kid came back to her and said he knew why he couldn't keep a job. He didn't have good work skills. This is something that gets overlooked. Kids need to be taught the skills they need to succeed in life. In urban areas, and among many poor black students, the communication is street slang, and that's not the language the world speaks. The worlds of economics and success speak the standard American dialect. These kids need to learn how to communicate ideas in a professional, clear, efficient English language.

Poor Kids Can Learn TOO!

Have you ever noticed that people describe some black people as articulate? President Barak Obama is articulate. I've never heard anyone say that a white person is articulate. When people say a black man or woman is well spoken, that means the image of black people is that they don't speak well.

On the 2011 season of the Celebrity Apprentice, NeNe Leakes, of The Real Housewives of Atlanta, had a confrontational moment with Star Jones, lawyer and TV star. In this episode NeNe was offended by something Star said to her. She was out of control and couldn't control her mouth. Then she went to street mode, essentially challenges Star to a fight. This was on national TV. And NeNe was saying, "I'm gonna get street on you. And you ain't going to do nothing to me. …" She used profanity and was getting, for lack of a better term, ghetto. In Star's rebuttal, she said, "I want to show America how an educated black woman conducts themselves and talks and how an uneducated black woman talks and conducts themselves." Unreal. That is exactly what I'm talking about. The perception of black America and young black America is negative, largely because our communication skills and the way we wear our clothes – pants hanging off your tail, earrings, tattoos, clothes too big – are negative. We have been socially disconnected from the real world. We are not in a position to prosper and be successful, because we have socially and emotionally separated ourselves from the American world education system.

Many black poor people in urban areas get left behind because they don't know how to conduct themselves. They don't know how to meet emotional challenges. They don't do good business or don't put their best foot forward in times of crisis and challenge. We typically revert to where we're comfortable, and that's something we need to work on. That's something that, in an urban education model, we have to address. Our students have to know that there is a social methodology about how whites work in America, and you've got to socially meet that challenge. You cannot back down or say, "Well I'm gonna do what I wanna do and I want to be myself." Basically, you're taking an oath of poverty, and it's been proven that, socially, we don't know how to compete. This is why we must engage our students in a curriculum of social education. Learning how to compete and communicate in life, and how to live on a successful plane.

That is irrefutable. We do not have to live a certain way because we're black. "I'm keeping it real." None of that mess. I learned how to play the game. I learned how to communicate. I learned how to view life. I learned how to view money. I learned how to view marriage. I learned how to view my health. I know what's good and healthy for me; I know what to do. That's the type of education we must engage in our K through 12 education process. As the black family has decomposed, the need for social education has increased. Our Title I parents have not given us the education we need, thus we need it from our schools.

9. Urban Title I schools must socially educate and develop black male students.

The number one cause of death of African Americans ages 15 to 29 is homicide. The majority of all special education students are boys and a large percent in urban areas are black boys. Most of our discipline problems are black boys. One study in Chicago said that one out of every fourth African American boy in Chicago public schools got expelled last year. The data says that boys are 80 percent more likely to drop out, and that they take up less than 50 percent of all college enrollment.

What does this mean? Our urban city boys are not being prepared for the world. They don't know how to socially compete. The education system is moving too slowly for their minds, and they're choosing paths of better interest and things that hold their attention such as street activity, crime, gangs, drugs, sex and a supreme interest in making money. We have to meet the needs and interest of our boys. Our boys have lost interest in school, and it's because it does not minister to their needs. Learning needs and styles of boys are absolutely different. You cannot continue to teach boys on the same level as girls, and that is particularly true for black boys. Black boys have a different learning ability. All of us who work in Title I schools know this. We see that communicating with black boys is different, and their ability to understand you is different. **They are more connected to their emotional intelligence and how they feel.** It is a self-esteem battle to work with young black boys in urban cities.

We have to cater our professional development programs toward the needs of African American boys. **Students who learn differently don't need after-school programs to learn. They need accurate during-school instruction.** After-school programs are OK, but they are replacing general education because so many black boys have lost interest in regular education. It does not stimulate them. Many after-school programs are a part of the problem because they don't solve the learning needs of the boys. School has to be interesting or many black boys are not going to go. That's true for both boys and girls. School has to be alive. Using technology, hands-on learning and engaging discussions will appeal to black boys. Why? They "feel" a part of the experience. Passing out handouts and reading assignments with no comprehension, no discussion, no instructional time, these are proven bad learning methods for African American boys. Black boys can learn. They are not stupid savages. However, the one-size-fits-all method is a complete failure in the urban area. Boys need more hands on, one-on-one interaction.

As the father of three children, one daughter and twins boys, I have long said that men are more emotional than woman. All my research and work experience, and now parenting experience, fully confirms this. My daughter loves her dad, loves to be with her dad and learn in multiple facets. However, my sons require a different approach. My daughter can take discipline and correction and bounce right back. My sons need more nurturing through the process to protect their fragile male egos and confidence. I have found this to be completely true at all male ages and stages. The male ego is delicate and must be managed with care. I have often said that society does not understand men, and my research and experience in the field of education supports this whole heartedly. Our understanding of the male ego has caused millions of black boys and men to quit education. With their confidence shaken and their pride acting as a barrier to common sense, many boys quit. And others get pushed through the system, without the skills and ability to read or write.

When I was a teenager, I went to an urban high school in Detroit. I was not a behavior problem, and the teachers liked me, but I didn't have the basic skills needed to be successful in life. I graduated with about a 2.9. I got 3.0 very frequently. I was an average student. I did OK on my work, but I did not have mastery of basic skills. However, my teachers passed me anyway. I remember being in 11th grade and getting an A in English. **When I graduated from high school, I could not read or write.** I went to a community college for my first college experience, and in my first college class I encountered the English teacher from hell. The first day of class the teacher asked if we'd write an impromptu page about our summer and ourselves. I remember doing the assignment with great enthusiasm. The class was on a Tuesday and Thursday. I returned for the next class on Thursday and the instructor gave me my paper back with a fat F in red and a devil head, and it said "see me."

I went to see her after class. I was totally frazzled and didn't know what it meant. The teacher, who was a white woman, said to me, "You might want to consider working with your hands because college is not for you." She had a concerned look on her face. My heart was racing and I fought back the tears. This was a heart-breaking statement for a young black man with an already low self-esteem and fragile confidence. She said this based on one paper, and having never met me before. She made an assessment that college was not for me. It was heartbreaking. I actually cried when I left class. I asked whether there was anything I could do to work on my skills. She said yes, but that I'd have to do a lot of work, and "I don't think it's possible."

She said I could get a tutor and have somebody proofread my work and help me to write better. So, for the next six years, that's what I did. I worked on my craft. I went to see tutors. I constantly worked. I went to teachers, asked for feedback and learned to proofread. I gained better control of the English language and learned the power of the dictionary. Thank God for spell check. That's how I got through my first college degree. And I just continued to get better. I continued to work on it at my master's level. I continued to work on it on my Ph.D. level. I continued to work on it 20 books later. Just being better, working harder and learning my craft. It's something I stayed committed to. I never have been or will be a quitter. I will never stop working on my skills. I started the day that teacher tried to steal my dream of being a college graduate and being a success in life.

This is an example of why we have to understand that boys are different. Parents have to understand it, teachers have to understand it, and school districts have to understand it. We have to stop introducing information and models that put all kids in the same category. We need professional experts in education who understand and have worked with African-American boys, who are African-American men, who have sons who are African-American boys, who help other African-American boys and men, and who teach African-American boys. This is what I've seen work best. This is why I've made my own models based off my data and research and professional experience.

Millions of young black men are making decisions every day about whether to stay in school and go to college or give up and go to prison. The urban education system must be aggressive in addressing this problem in the classroom, not with after-school programs.

10. Urban Title schools must help 100 percent of all of our parents become GED holders or high school graduates.

This step is critical to advance the education agenda. Over the next 5 years, every Title I school in America needs to make this a reality. Every one of our parents should complete their requirements for a GED or high school diploma. This is not negotiable.

Ignorance and lack of education fuel poverty. This is where the comeback of the economy is going to come from. More than 80 percent of all welfare recipients, and free and reduced lunch parents don't have a high school diploma. That tells you what the problem is. You can't get away from the real problem and come up with other programs. They want to educate/program people who don't have an education, and it's not going to work.

We have to challenge all parents to rise to a new level. We cannot challenge students without also challenging parents. You can't have theoretical parent liaisons or poverty exploiting organizations that manipulate parents and play on their ignorance or poverty, offering kickbacks to support their program. I have seen many urban Title I programs use parents to get programs at their school and receive improper jobs and cash. It's all kickback. That's why the urban school has been ruined. Everybody's trying manipulate the system. This is unethical and often creates situations in which parents and students do not receive the best services. This is not OK. I remember working with a parent while providing services in several Title I schools. This woman was a theoretically powerful parent, and head of a parent association. This woman got it into her head that I had a lot of money. She asked me to do seminars for her parent group. The bill was probably about $4,500 for seminars with books. Then she came back to me and asked me to give her $600.00 to send her daughter on a trip to Orlando with the school. Once

I realized that I was being shook down, I told her that our company didn't make personal donations, but we could make a donation to the school. This woman went on to blacklist me among some Title I parents. This woman was saying that "I charge too much money," "I'm not truthful," "I'm a liar." She went on to tell a lot of lies about me.

In this same district, the major problem is kids dropping out because of incarceration. Well, another woman who was part of the parent group for the district knew about us but rejected our services. The following summer, her son got locked up. It was his first time; he was busted in a robbery and is serving four years in prison. After he got caught up in the system, this woman started calling me to ask whether I had any connections. She wanted her son's time reduced and for him to be moved him closer to home. The irony is this woman said that she wanted me to do a seminar on keeping kids out of prison, but continually criticized me for my prices. This was the same woman who ended up hiring another provider who charged three times my rate, and she influenced many other parents to do the same. **We later found out that the provider had a friend that provided frequent kickbacks. This lady manipulated naïve parents against what they needed and used Title I budgeted money to do so.** This is in a district that sends the government back millions in unused Title I funds every year.

Most Title I parents are not equipped to do this level of work. Having parents as president of the PTO, the PTA and a part of the Title I group is

Poor Kids Can Learn TOO!

not a good idea. Most are not equipped to govern. You might put a parent in charge of a $25,000 Title I budget and they might have an income of $500 a month. It is difficult to think in a prosperous manner with an income of $500 month. A prosperous mind is needed to help Title I students and parents to change their situation. Many PTA presidents might say, "I'm not paying $5,000 for a seminar. That's too much money. We can get this guy to do it for $500." or "$50 is too much to pay for a book." Well, in their world it is. But ask yourself, why is it too much money, especially when it comes to giving your child an advantage in their education. When you're dealing with education and investing in your children, it's never too much money. But for impoverished people, it is. This is why our parents need help. This is why our first initiative must be to bring 100 percent of all parents to complete a GED or high school diploma. Second, we must help them to be better leaders in the business of education. You're not a good leader if you're trying to get kickbacks, or don't know how to allocate a Title I budget. This means learning how to obtain the best (not most cost efficient) services for your money.

I'm reminded of an outstanding parent at Detroit Cass Technical High School. Ms. Frances Billingsley heard about our services and approached me. She said she needed help working with boys. In fact, many of the teachers at our schools struggle in working with young boys. She also wanted to make sure her son's needs were met at her school. She thought our services were a perfect fit. Not one time did she fret about the price. She was not concerned about those things. She went on to connect the services with the principal of the school, and we conducted several professional development and parent development seminars there. The evaluations from teachers and parents indicated that our sessions were some of the best they had experienced. Why? We met the needs of the people.

Money is not the issue. Just take care of your business, find the best people you can, and do what's best for the kids. Francis Billingsley of Detroit, MI., at Cass Technical High School, is a great example of that. An awesome person who cares and knows what her population needed.

11. Urban Title I schools must find, develop and retain talented and willing professionals.

The biggest problem in the Title I system is that the staff is ill prepared and misinformed of the challenges of urban education. People who work in urban education have to be trained at a different level. As a holder of four college degrees, I can honestly say that college did not prepare me for working with students and parents in an urban setting. Fundamentally, the education system does not account for the differences in urban areas. The system is committed to a one-size-fits-all model. This is evident from the policies that are enforced. **Making test scores a primary benchmark for identified learning progress is a colossal error.** Many schools have mastered teaching kid's test-taking skills as part of the curriculum. In urban schools that confront social issues on a daily basis, educational progress must be measured differently.

Urban educators have to make education come alive to students. This calls for special people with special skills, and we need more professional development. Oftentimes, the biggest issue in education is that you have good teachers who love kids but who don't have a comprehensive understanding the urban life and its affect on students. So you have a situation where we are Ill-equipped to deal with the kids' needs where we work.

Let's take, for example, a man coaching girls basketball. I've coached girls and boys basketball, and I realize that girls and boys had different needs. When I coached girls, I always had women on my staff. Why? Because the needs of those young women are different. When the young girls had their monthly menstrual cycle and we're practicing, they were going through all type of changes. This required a different understanding that I did not have. I had to learn about the needs of the people I work with, and it's the same thing in education. We cannot neglect the needs of the people we serve. If our students are hungry, we have to feed them. In education today, there's neglect based on a lack of understanding, whether social or emotional. Many people who work in urban education environments are not cut out for it. It's the same as being a police officer in a city like Troy, Mich., or in Detroit – there are big differences. These fundamental differences have to be respected. The lifestyles and values are different. People are always trying to find similarities. "Oh, we're the same," or "Oh, I relate." But a lot of times, we don't relate.

Poor Kids Can Learn TOO!

Again, one major difference in the urban education model is the paradigm shift between sympathy and empathy. Sympathy is a cancer to the education system. You can't sympathize with your students because you have to teach them, but you can empathize – "I imagine that must be painful, but here is what we are going to do." "I imagine it must be tough to grow up with a mother who is a crack head." "I can imagine it must be tough to grow up without your father." My head can't even wrap around some of the things these kids in urban districts go through. So you're going to have to operate at a much higher level.

You're not helping them if you're ill-prepared and don't relate. Our basic education training does not cover urban education issues, such as hunger, poverty, housing, sexual conduct, substance abuse, domestic abuse, learning deficiencies and poor health. These issues get neglected. We cannot teach people and gain their respect while neglecting their core issues. That's like being the doctor of a cancer patient and saying you are going to treat the cancer, but not help with your diet. That's neglect of the worst kind. And that's what we have happening here. This is why professional development in the urban areas must be improved. One of my colleagues said that before he started working there, his district hadn't had professional development in 10 years. Can you believe that? The district might have had a personal development day, but nothing was in place to help professionals improve services to urban students. That is dangerous. That means no growth. That means freestyle teaching. You get teacher who doesn't know what they're doing, and they will make it up as they go along.

My middle school English teacher was a pastor of a church. He used to talk to us, but he didn't teach us anything about English. Instead, he preached to us every day. He used to talk to us about going to prison. But he used to say, "The way y'all act, you gonna go to prison. And you know what they gonna do to you in prison? They gonna screw you in your rectum." Now, he is a good man and he saved my soul. I came to the Lord due to fear of prison. However, he didn't teach us a lick of English. These antics continued through high school due to lazy unskilled teachers. That's why I graduated without those skills, and struggled so much in college. I know from back in the day that professional development days were like days off for teachers. There was no learning going on. The worst thing a teacher can do is stop learning. Educators must be like business people, always learning. Teachers should go to professional and personal development classes once a month, but they should not be forced to do it. They should go because they are lifelong learners, and learners are earners. Learners and educators change the world. You can't get caught stagnated with the issues of life, and not perfect your craft. Can you imagine being a boxer and not training? Can you imagine being a basketball player and not going to the gym to work on your shots? Can you imagine being a bodybuilder who works out only once a month or once a year? Are you delusional? That's what millions of teachers are doing, and that's why we have an under-performing school system.

Our teachers have not gotten an efficient education or the right education, and then it hasn't been ongoing. Many of the professional development programs today do not interest the staff because they do not address the issues and needs of the staff.

Teachers go to personal development days, but they hang out in their classrooms, writing notes, balancing their checkbook, text messaging, making a grocery list. They're doing everything but learning. That's why our professional development trainings for teachers have been consistently rated the number one professional development program for urban teachers. We address the needs of the people, providing relevant quality professional development training that honestly addresses the needs, issues and concerns of teachers and the needs of students and parents. We need to be honest with our teachers about what's going on. They have to be valued, loved and appreciated. We have to create an environment in which our teachers can grow and become next level educators and not be stifled in their growth and development of life.

We've got to recruit the best, and we've got to pay the best. We have to sell our teachers on the mission of education. If you are in a district that promises to be competitive, if you respect people and if you create an environment where people can learn and get better, people will come and work for you, even if your wage is not be the top of the scale. Educators want to work an environment where they will grow and develop. Many professionals will take a chance and go to an urban district if they can actually teach and do what they need to do to be successful. No educator wants to continuously be dumped on and cursed at in staff meetings, making them feel worse than they already do. These are things that we don't need. This is what creates strife in urban education settings.

12. All urban Title I schools must have strong business partnerships and sponsorships of corporate entities and faith-based organizations. All urban schools must have the backing of some financial power. You have to be able to connect to corporate America as well as local businesses. You need to maintain a sponsorship that allows you to connect with structures where they can model success. We have to gain an understanding through our connection with the corporate world concerning the importance of post secondary education. Preparing for life and other situations is a vital skill for our students. Urban Title I schools have to gain the support of people with serious resources. You need millionaires and professional athletes who have the money to sponsor things you need to have done, and who can give your kids jobs when they graduate from school. These are critical components to being educated and having a powerful urban education institution.

This builds the culture of success when people say we are partners with GM or Ford. I know one high school in Michigan that has a partnership with Fed-Ex. Through this partnership, juniors and seniors can get part-time jobs making $10 per hour and learn about the corporate structure in America. Plenty of corporate entities want to be a part of the community and make a contribution in a positive and productive manner. These partnerships give students hope and something to look forward to, and they give the district great credibility for offering opportunities for its students outside of the classroom. It's called real-world experience, and it's what makes a powerful school system. No longer can urban Title I students be left behind because they don't have the opportunities that other kids have. These opportunities are created in an emotional and social environment. This balances the playing field by playing the game. The education system is different. You cannot compare suburban education, rural education and urban education. **Urban education is different, and that needs to be better understood.**

This is the model of urban education for Title I schools. This is the proven system that will allow us to be more effective and give our students and parents an opportunity to be successful in every area of life. This model addresses the needs of our students and it addresses the needs of our professionals. Head on, it meets all needs of the urban school system with no excuses. If you can find a way to operate under this model at all times, I guarantee you will have a more stable, productive and consistently successful outcome for your Title I students and parents.

Every student can learn, just
not on the same day, or the
same way.
-- George Evans

Chapter 6
12 Power Methods To Teach And Work With Title I Students and Parents

1. Make education relevant.
A power method for helping impoverished students and parents must be to make education relevant. Helping people understand poverty and how to get out of it must be a frequent part of their education process. This requires knowledge and new information. Too many poor black and Hispanic children, particularly boys, are totally disinterested with school because it's not relevant to their life. It's not relevant to the things they are dealing with and addressing in their life. When a person does not have money, they think about that all day long. So the onus is on us to make education relevant to the student's situation. Education has to be relevant to their life, not the life you think is important. When working with Title I students and parents, we have to reach back and pull them forward. We have to start with them on their level, not your level. This is why so many professionals from different economic social classes struggle with working with economically disadvantage students and parents. They cannot relate and refuse to come down off their imaginary high horse. That is why they are miserable and have so many problems with the students and parents. If this is you, change your attitude or change schools. If you are not going to make education relevant to the world in which your students live and are not going to become empathetic (confrontational and challenging) but

remain sympathetic (passive), you will not be effective and school will remain boring.

2. Acknowledge cultural history.

In situations where you have a significant population of minority students and parents, it is critical to acknowledge cultural backgrounds and differences. It is wise to show respect for ethnic differences. Black, Hispanic, Arab American, Chaldean group differences, cultural beliefs and attitudes must be addressed and managed openly, not in private or under the table. One of the serious problems in the Title I community is the inability to address issues of race in a positive and productive manner. Race and culture are major characteristics that make students who they are. Engaging cultural competencies in the education process is necessary to empower the students. To minority students and parents, race is always a factor. They might not verbalize it or admit it when confronted, but it definitely plays a role in their mindset. Discussing history is important if you don't want them to repeat it. To guarantee that somebody keeps doing the same thing, hide them from their history. If you want to promote success and change while teaching Title I students and parents, you've got to implement cultural history and understanding. Black history, Hispanic history, and history of poverty are important to impoverished people. Implementing the discussion of history to current day events will bring it alive for a young person so they can identify, know and have a basis for how they can deal with it and make changes.

3. Superior classroom control.

Many times in Title I schools, classroom control and management are severely lacking. A lot of educators are not able to manage the personalities the classroom. Many of our students do not have proper supervision at home; therefore, they have not learned how to conduct themselves in a classroom. Because of their behavioral problems in the classrooms, many boys are referred for special education when they need discipline, training and instruction. This is where strong educators come into play. We need educators who know what behavior is unacceptable and can stand up to students. We need teachers to return to no tolerance during class and command the respect of their students. When students don't respect a teacher and frequently disrupt the classroom, it is because they feel they can.

Some students have no respect for the education process, and it is a reflection of the parent. However, educators must demand respect through consistency of boundaries and expectations. I have seen many teachers allow students in their personal space, trying not to offend the student. This is totally wrong. All correction must be done in love, but no teacher can ever allow a student to disrupt the learning process for other students. True classroom management is about classroom presence. Classroom presence is about ownership – taking control and responsibility over what belongs to you, and that is your classroom. For a teacher, the classroom must be as sacred as your home. The boundaries of your home must be built and protected; the same is true for the classroom. **Title I educators must toughen up.** Stop acting like wimps who are afraid of children. You cannot show fear, at any time. If you're going to be afraid or you don't like the people you serve, you're in the wrong field.

Title I students, the economically disadvantaged, are often raised in a "renter" mentality and they have a lack of respect for their property and others.

1) So the first principal of classroom management is teaching and demanding respect for the classroom.

2) Secondly, teachers must have respect for the students. Many of our students do have behavioral problems and lack respect for authority. However, this should not impact your ability to provide education services. This requires great maturity. You cannot teach a student who you don't respect.

3) Third, you've got to understand the student's background and upbringing. Many of our students were not raised like us; therefore, we must come outside of ourselves to truly serve Title I students and parents.

4) Fourth, you must have empathy for the student. Again empathy, not sympathy. This means you have to know more about your students than ever before to make the learning process work. It requires that you learn how to build a relationship with your students, with direct communication. It is going to require more time. This is a non-traditional method that teachers

and educators must use to address issues in the 21st century. It takes time to get to know people. It is particularly true when the students and parents are so guarded. Students might say they don't know you or "why do you want to know?" This increases the need for relationship building skills. Students can sense a lack of sincerity.

5) You've got to have the ability to adjust because things will not always go well. If I'm going to manage a classroom, I've got to be able to adjust.

6) Maximize your space. I have seen many classrooms that are cluttered. Don't be afraid to adjust and move desks around. Stop junking and pack-ratting in the classroom. Get that crap out of there and use that space to move young people around your classroom. Most males are movement learners.

7) Celebrate all victories. On a day-to-day or week-to-week basis, celebrating victories and being able to highlight progress with these students is huge. You're contributing and building self-esteem, and all of our students need that.

8) Don't let up. Never negotiate with a Title I student or parent. You've got to be a holder of policy and structure because, typically in Title I situations, manipulation is major. So it's important that you have frequent intervention and communication with the parents to avoid this dynamic.

9) You need rules and structure. All classrooms should have the rules posted, and there should be no more than 5 to 7 rules. Keep it basic. They should be posted and they must stick with your structure. You've got to have structure. You've got to have a lesson plan, but you also must be able to be flexible with it. Structure is what increases the learning of young people. This is the way you must manage the Title I classroom of the 21st century.

4. Acknowledge and address social factors.
Social factors can include an individual's home life, their nutrition, delinquent family history, where they live, family gang involvement, sleeping habits, where they sleep (do they have a bed or sleep on the floor), etc. These are all factors that become relevant in urban education with Title I students. If you don't know these types of precious details, you could be in a situation where students are unproductive and it's self-defeating to your goals as an educator. If you don't have all the data, you don't know how to address the problems.

5. Use visual and audio aids.
When you're teaching Title I students today, you have to use visual aids. Even though the students are economically disadvantaged, they have an abundance of exposure to television, radio, media, DVDs, and movies. Students are clearly interested in TV, social media and other visual aids, so take advantage of it. To break those molds in the Internet generation, where elementary school kids are text

messaging, taking pictures and these types of things, you must be able to adjust, set structure and use that to your advantage. You can't buckle and crumble under the pressure and say, "Well I don't like this," and "We're not doing that," and "I'm going to stick to my handouts." That's a bad idea. These are ideas that don't improve student learning. They don't create a situation in which the student is challenged or inspired to learn. Students are not enjoying the learning process because we are not tapping into their personal interests. Learning can and should be fun. If you want to increase Title I students' academic interests and abilities, you're going to have to tap into it, and visual aids is one of the key ways you can do that.

6. Group activity.
I have found that in the social media form of life, many of our students are engaged in the group aspect of life. Then they go to school, and it becomes an individualistic approach. What I have found productive in working with incarcerated males is making learning group-orientated, where students can engage in ideas as a group and cognitively process the information as a group. You get a lot better outcome. Life is a team sport. We've got to stop training kids as individuals. In the world of family, business and economics, people strive to build strong teams. Yes, you do have to be personally accountable for yourself, but people with low self-esteem or low achievers have got to be put in groups where they can work together. Being accountable to one another builds morale. It's like

playing on a team. We learn to play for something bigger than ourselves. Low achieving students will work better in groups. When they see someone in a group doing well, it motivates them to want to do well. Title I educators have to practice tapping into the power of group work and activities, and helping students to work together for a common goal to bring down social walls – whether that means graduating to the fifth grade, reading, working on a group presentation or going to college. Group learning is effective if used correctly.

7. Presentation learning.
Presentation learning is the ability to teach others what you have learned. It is important to introduce young people to giving presentations. Many Title I students and parents lack the ability to communicate efficiently and appropriately. Educators must place emphasis on training and teaching Title I students and parents how to communicate in front of a group. Being able to give presentations and present information is a valuable skill that will stay with them the rest of their lives. It is especially important to encourage boys to get involved, give speeches and make presentations because all men want to look good. They want to get out there and beat the other guy. Boys are competitive, and I believe it is important to tap into the spirit of competition. Life is competitive. Business is competitive. Boys have to be prepared for the real world, and presentations can help to do that.

8. Students and parents must be seen as partners.

In the 21st century, you want to start looking at the student and parent as one. Oftentimes you hear people say, it's all about the kids. While it is about the kids, in the 21st century, it's all about students and parents. You can't say you're trying to help the students and not attempt to empower the parents. I've asked every Title I school in America to make it their initiative to help all the parents there to obtain a GED or high school diploma. For a Title I parent, getting a GED or working on their high school diploma in an accelerated program in the community is the most important thing they can do. We cannot continue to promote education to the child, while the parent is illiterate with low self-esteem and feels major embarrassment. We can't let that happen, and as teachers, principals and coordinators, our number one goal must be to help our students and parents see themselves in a better position than they are. The only way to do that is to lovingly make it mandatory that parents get their GED or high school diploma. Lovingly Mandatory – this is my initiative throughout this country, helping Title I parents achieve their basic educational requirements and start the journey toward post-secondary education. This is only way to help a Title I family.

Basic education credentials change the way people see themselves and their ability to get employed. The reason why my M.A.N School treatment program for incarcerated youth has been so successful is because it's mandatory that they get a GED or a high school diploma before being released. That is one major step in not re-offending and getting back into negative behavior. Where literacy and basic education requirements (GED or high school diploma) are not met, poverty abounds. The new Title I standard has got to be 100 percent of Title I parents getting a GED or high school diploma. This will influence the learning of the students. That's the only way to go from disadvantage to advantage. If we're saying that education is the key, and the parent doesn't have the education, then we're failing and we cannot continue to fail like that. This must be addressed. This is our agenda for the next 20 years. My goal is to help schools make sure 100 percent of the parents have a GED or high school diploma. This will change the culture of Title I students and parents, forever. If you know that your school or district needs help in this regards, contact me and I will help you get it done.

9. Conduct a promotion program for all grade levels. Having a promotion celebration for all grade levels is a remarkable incentive for students to do well. Student achievement for Title I students must be frequently celebrated. Poverty does cause a gap in many of our students' and parents' self-esteem; therefore, providing a minor celebration for all grades is major. The goal is constant love, encouragement and positive reinforcement. A Title I student and parent should experience yearly promotions/graduations. When they know promotion with a celebration is planned at the end of every year, no one will want to get left behind. With Title I students and parents, that's the way you have to do it because we're in the **right now gratification era**. If we could start celebrating promotion on all levels, it will greatly increase parental involvement because they know at the end of the year; they will be celebrated for doing well. All of us know that Title I parents will come out to celebrate their children. So let us take advantage of that. That'll give us the best results.

10. Work on a pace system.

I've always believed that students who learn more quickly or slowly should be separated in an ethical way so no one's learning gets stunted. A lot of boys may learn at a different pace; however, it is not a reason to refer them for special education. Their learning style might be different. If a person is learning more quickly and adapting the information, you've got to separate them from the other student for the good of all the students. One, you want the student who is getting it to keep moving. And two, you want students who might be struggling to stay focused and can get the resources needed to be successful. The pace method will be effective in helping students in this predicament.

In addition to focusing the pace of learning, teachers simply need more time for instruction. We're held to a standard, where we have got to get 12 months worth of work done in 8 ½ months. We don't have enough instruction time. That's a fact. Somehow, someway, in your school and district, you've got to address that and come up with a way to beat it. It must be addressed, whether it is by changing to a 12-month school year with more breaks, or giving a $20,000 or more a year raise for all teachers and administrators and overtime for after-school learning for teachers, or both.

11. You've got to separate behavior problems.
There's a difference between the lack of the ability to learn and a behavior problem. A behavior problem has to be separated. Now, all behavior problems should not mean kicking the student out of school. Many behavior problems can be skillfully addressed in school, but in a classroom with a teacher who is skilled at managing these behaviors and who can teach students while they are managing their behaviors. Students with disruptive behaviors cannot be allowed to disrupt the learning process, and it's our job to make sure it's not happening. The key is that kids want to learn, but they need the right environment to learn. That means we know the difference between behavioral problems and special education. Students who are developmentally disabled and students who have anti-personality disorder should not be in the same classroom. Anti-personality disorder students have some behavioral issues; they're not happy children. They like to be disruptive, but they should not be in a special education classroom. They need a special behavioral learning classroom with a powerful teacher. This distinction will improve the quality of our classrooms and the quality of our schools overall.

12. Promote post-secondary education.

One of the major pieces in Title I student and parent education is the promotion of post-secondary education. One of the ways you can change the life of the economically disadvantaged student is to introduce him to post-secondary education opportunities at an early age. We have to show young people the things that life has to offer and the paths they need to take to get there at an early age. No students in this world are going to advance without access to higher levels of education. I have always said and branded the statement that "college is for everyone, but a college degree is not." Everybody has to have the opportunity to go to college and to experience the empowering social college environment. The social factors in that college environment create a situation that gives young people opportunities and choices they have not had before. When you're raised in poverty, you tend to believe the world is small, but the college experience (even one class) can change that. A lot of teachers have given students negative ideas about education and post secondary education because they may have not performed at a high level in K-12. And what I have found is that means very little to a student's overall ability to adapt to the college life and learning style. Many times the college environment will empower an underachieving student to achieve. Post-secondary education gives people a chance to connect to the new world. Regardless of what field you're going into, whether you need a college degree or not, one college class can change your life. Why is it that 8 of the 10

Poor Kids Can Learn TOO!
73

richest people in American all went to college and dropped out? The environment fueled their ambition, and once they were ready, they left school. You don't have to get a degree. That's where a lot of the bad information's coming, and a lot of Title I students have had their dreams stolen. "Well, you know, college isn't for everybody. Get in a job training program," they say. Ladies and gentlemen, let me ask you, where are they cutting today? Jobs. So why would we send another generation in the direction that they sent a lot of us and it didn't work for us. Hundreds of my colleagues are out of work with master's and Ph.D.'s. That advice didn't work. That is not the automatic system of success. A lot of us have ended up in situations where we haven't had the life we wanted. We got talked out of it. Somebody told us, "Oh, no. That won't work. Don't do that. You won't be able to do this or that." These ideas are not winning ideas. What I found with this generation is when you are trying to get somebody out of poverty, you have to coach them at the extreme difference. That means you can't coach the man in poverty to just get a job and to do a little bit better. Why? The poverty mind will say, "It is better to stay home and just collect my disability or collect my assistance. They're going to give it to me. It's not a lot but I'm not working for it." The poverty mind is content with a little. They have to be coached to believe that something better is possible. We have got to coach them to be entrepreneurs or high-earning professional such accountants. They need to know that they can go to a higher level in life, that they can live the impossible. The problem has come when most teachers have not maximized their potential and lived the life they wanted. Someone took most of our dreams, and it is time to take them back. Teachers and principals have to believe that you can dream and live it, that a poor, fat kid from Detroit, MI, can find his passion, live his dream, do the work he loves and become a millionaire business owner. All things are possible for those who believe and act. In this new world of technology and social media, everyone who has a dream and desire coupled with effort has a shot. Success is no longer promised to the student who goes to school, gets good grades, goes to college, and hopes it works out. Today, that advice is a rolling of the dice. If you say, well I want to be an entrepreneur or entertainer, I think you have about the same chance of success with that plan. Technology has balanced the playing field. The emergence of the Internet and youtube.com has got kids becoming millionaires over the Internet. With the emergence of these powerful tools, teachers and principals need to be educated on the new world and how to create a better life and product for our students.

The challenge of educating the economically disadvantaged Title I student and parent is a great task. However, it's completely doable. It's doable with new education. It's doable with professional staff, teachers and principals who are willing to learn new skills, the skill of motivation, the skill of innovation, the skill of going back and helping students reconnect to their passions and dreams. **No**

longer will we be able to inspire young people based on fear. This generation has no fears. They cannot be punked into doing what we think is right. **They have to be taught, challenged, redirected, modeled by educators living what their preaching, and consistently inspired. Kids today are inspired by the ability to dream, not the fear of failure.** They feel like they're failures already so you can't scare them into success. It reminds me of programs like "Scared Straight." Those things never worked. They gave students negative mental imagery, but they didn't keep students from being unsuccessful. They scared students from going to jail, but made them dormant in another passion or form in life. We should not want to scare our students; we should want to empower them. We don't want to alienate our parents; we should want to challenge, empower and support our parents in their endeavors to raise children in the 21st century. It's a great challenge. It's very difficult. **Parents need a tremendous amount of support.** Today's Title I parent is looking to teachers, principals and juvenile justice judges for guidance, because most are not equipped to provide that guidance. Our staffs are going to have to be totally retrained in the next 3 years to the new Title I model. Everybody's got to be retrained to be able attack this problem head-on, with new, strong ideas that are going to inspire students and parents to step up and meet the challenge of poverty. Poverty can be eradicated only with knowledge that produces wealth. Poverty cannot be met with poverty. An impoverished man in the mind and spirit cannot help a man who is impoverished in the mind, spirit and pocket.

Colleagues, we are going to have to make personal changes in our lives and grow. This book was about the personal changes you have to make within yourself. This is why I've created my professional development program and made it available to every school in America. Retraining Title I professionals with the skills and understanding needed to efficiently help the 21st century Title I student and parent, and helping schools and professionals deal with the most difficult and tough issues in Title I education is critical. Take advantage of this awesome, powerful professional development series. Bring it to your school to empower the staff. Don't get caught ill prepared by not being proactive and preparing your staff for the challenge of helping the economically disadvantaged students with the empowering knowledge that they can succeed and don't have to be poor all their lives. There is no shortage in the world's wealth, there's only a shortage in the knowledge and ideas of how to bring it into their lives. Our greatest asset is our mind and empowered loving teachers. That means you. Title I students and parents are counting on us to be prepared to meet this challenge. This country is counting on you to give the economically disadvantaged an opportunity, a glimpse of hope, and an action plan to prevent them from living in poverty the rest of their lives. I empower you, my colleague, to do this job, which is very difficult, but never impossible.

Dr. Jesse W. Jackson III

Poor Kids Can Learn TOO!

Dr. Jesse W. Jackson III

Parents

Versus

Teachers

How To Decrease Parent And Teacher Conflict

Poor Kids Can Learn TOO!

Introduction

During the age of the No Child Left Behind movement, the relationship between parents and teachers has dissolved. It has become clear that we have two separate agendas. Parents are trying to maintain their integrity, and oftentimes, teachers are covering their tails. To help put an end to this divisive rivalry, I have developed some basic conflict resolution principles for both teachers and parents. I hope these ideas can help us to work better as a team and end the conflict.

It is widely believed that this conflict hurts only the students, and this is not true. This ongoing conflict and division actually destroy both parties, because their conscience stays burdened with negative thoughts and feelings. I have ruled strife and division a cancer to the human spirit and the education system. Parents, teachers should be your best friends. And teachers, parents are your greatest asset. No longer can we afford to continue this foolish pride-driven battle. Everyone, it is time to grow up and be more professional. Parents and teachers must take responsibility for improving this relationship. Here are some basic do's and don'ts for parents and teachers to improve the relationship.

Chapter 1
Parent Conflict Prevention Plan

1. Parents must never confront a teacher.
Parents are welcome to ask questions of the teachers, but they should not visit the school in the name of "checking on the teacher" with a hostile posture. This type of confrontation is not productive. It creates a negative school environment and it puts you in a negative light. It would be beneficial to take a neutral party with you to talk to a teacher if you think you cannot have a positive rapport with the teacher. Exchanging negative words back and forth is immature and unprofessional.

2. Know your rights as a parent.
Parents are an essential part of the education process. Title I legislation specifically states that parents must be part of budgeting and school planning. Parents have to know about the resources available, not only to help students, but to parents in the educational process. It's important for parents to know their rights, and that means they must be involved. You must open books and come to meetings.

3. Respect all staff.
Parents must not be disrespectful to secretaries, principals or teachers. They should respect everyone in the building and treat them as adults. Treat them as you would want to be treated.

4. Don't gossip and speak negatively about staff, especially in front of your child.

First, it is immature to bad mouth people, particularly when they are not present. Secondly, gossip and negative speaking are contagious, and children pick up on that and do the same thing. It increases the conflict between parents and students. Stop gossiping and using negative words toward professional staff.

5. Do not believe your child.

In case you are ill-informed, children lie. It is normal for all children to misrepresent the truth at some point. You must understand what's going on and process information without misrepresentation by your child. It will come back in the end to make you look foolish, and make you look like you don't know what you're talking about. Never believe your child without investigating first. As I say, trust, but verify.

6. Know your child's learning style.

Parents have to know their child's ability to learn. You've got to know how your child grasps information. A lot of times, teachers and students don't mix in terms of their learning styles and abilities. So parents have to know whether their children are audio, visual or hands-on learners. That means they need to be part of a learning experience. This is critical, particularly with boys. Knowing this is half the battle. Knowing this can help parents get their children's needs met and prevent conflict.

7. Do not make threats or challenges.

Civilized adults do not threaten or challenge teachers. It is immature, not to mention criminal, and it implies that you are not serious about a good outcome for your child. You have to manage negative events and conduct yourself as an adult if you want be respected. Do not yell or make a scene in the school. Many Title I parents tend to be younger with a low self-image, and tend to feed into that negative behavior. That type of conduct has no place in the educational setting. It's time for you to act your age, learn how to be professional and appropriate, and get the results you want. Yelling and screaming is juvenile and immature. You are a parent and you must act like one.

8. Keep your personal problems out of the schools.

Parents who have a problem with alcohol or drugs need to stay away from the school if they are drunk or high. Not only is this behavior an embarrassment to you and your child, it also opens the door to protective services allegations that you cannot manage your life and are out of control. Any respecting adult will call protective services if a parent is drinking or using drugs, then getting behind the wheel of a car and carrying a kid around. This shows that you have bad judgment. Do not bring personal problems or domestic issues to the school. It makes you look as if you're out of control and it ruins the child's reputation.

9. Make all complaints in writing.

Making complaints in writing gives you a time stamp and date so it can get resolved in a timely manner. If you make a complaint via email, always CC another party. Typically, when things are not in writing, they didn't happen. You don't want to practice telling someone, you want to practice putting it in writing to guarantee you have a paper trail and a record so things can get addressed in a timely manner.

10. Separate behavioral problems from developmental problems.

As a parent, you must identify whether your child has a behavior problem – whether the child has an antisocial personality, is dealing with a father not being in the house, or is frustrated, angry and fights a lot. Never let a behavioral problem get confused with a development problem. Special education is for those who are developmentally disabled, those who learn at a slower pace, not for behavior problems. They need special resources, maybe even medication. Developmentally disabled does not equal behavioral problem. For a lot of kids, behavioral problems mean the child needs love, a positive father, and frequent discipline. You don't want your child to be labeled as special ed because of their behavior. For more information of this topic, please read my book, *"College or Prison" How To Educate, Discipline And Keep Males In The Classroom & Out of Prison."*

11. Stay involved.

Don't take a year off from being involved with your child at school. You've got to be on top of it every step of the way. One bad week in school can cost you a 4-year scholarship. You want to make sure you never let these things get out of control. Parents must be on top of their children's education and there are no excuses or exceptions.

To decrease conflicts between parents and teachers, parents must become better people. I've always said that better people become better parents. Parents must grow up so they can be in a position to meet the emotional challenges of the 21st century. It is difficult being a parent today. What I'm asking all parents to do is to reflect on their upbringing and their relationship with their father. Look at the things that have hurt you and plan how you are going to address them going forward. What are you going to change so your life is different? You can't just say it will be different because you want it to be different. It will require different thoughts and different actions. If you want a different life for you and your child, it starts with you. Parents have to be more proactive in taking care of themselves. Parents who take care of themselves will not engage in frivolous conflicts and negative behavior with a teacher. They will learn that the teacher is their partner. The teacher is protecting their most important asset – their child.

Chapter 2
Teacher Conflict Prevention Plan

1. Acknowledge personal problems.
Teachers can help decrease conflicts with parents by acknowledging that many parents have personal problems. In the 21st century education system, teachers need to become more interested and aware of what's going on in the personal lives of students. It can no longer be "just come to school, learn then go home." What makes Title I different is that when a person is disadvantaged, there is a personal gap. Many times, these students have been neglected and look to their teachers for someone to talk to and someone to show them love, understanding and empathy. You never want to make excuses, but you need to be aware of the problems so you can manage the relationship with parents properly.

2. Respectfully address parents' issues.
Many Title I parents already feel inferior, so teachers should never portray an attitude that makes the parents feel belittled. Many times, Title I parents expect the worst and, even if a teacher does not suggest an inequality, they twist words so it appears the teacher is being disrespectful. Teachers need to practice how to respectfully take a step back because, a lot of times, parents will try to bombard us and engage us in a negative way. So we've got to stay a step ahead and always be respectful in the way we address them. You want to be assertive and respectfully address the issues while always staying professional.

3. Support parents' needs.

Increase the time and resources spent on supporting parents' needs, such as using Title I funds to help all parents get a GED or high school diploma. If you're trying to help parents, the best thing you can do is help parents on a personal level first, then you can help their children.

4. Keep parents informed.

I know a lot of good schools have parent email lists, and parents are always in the loop. Email is informative. Sending notes home with kids is prehistoric and doesn't work anymore. Look for more effective ways of communicating, whether it's uploading notes on Facebook or using the school's website. Keeping parents informed via text messages or email is very powerful and **gives the parent no excuses.** This also can prove to be helpful in what teachers are trying to do.

5. Understand the uniqueness of education.

Education is, first and foremost, a business, and that business side has been neglected for many years. People do not want to see education as a business, but it is. The thing that is unique is that your client is also your boss. Without students and parents, you have no company. They're not like customers who come to you to buy something or to eat, and they're happy to be here. A lot of times they are there by default. What you have to do is understand that uniqueness. When you understand that, you can perform better because it gives you a paradigm. You don't have to like that, but that's what makes education unique. And you have to manage that fact to be more productive and make the outcome more favorable for you.

6. Principals have to be very skilled in creating an environment of harmony and team.

Principals should never take sides, but always seek resolve and keep parents and teachers happy. This balance is critical in the education process. I specialize in consulting with principals and parent organizations to create a better working environment to improve student learning and academic achievement. If your school needs help in this area, call us 888-261-3412 or log onto www.thebestmancompany.com.

Parents and teachers have always been partners. Both parties rely on each other to do a job. Parents need teachers to educate their children, giving them a chance to be successful in life. And teachers need parents to support their efforts and respect their work. **When parents and teachers are not partners, the education system will not succeed.** Today, the parent-teacher relationship is the worst it has ever been. To change this, parents and teachers must once again come back to the table as partners. **Action step: Invite teachers to all parent meetings. Allow parent representatives to attend school staff meetings. This builds trust in the parent/ teacher relationship.**

Parents should be able to resolve all problems they might have with teachers. Parents should work with teachers and become their friend. It's not easy, but it is doable. And it requires you to make the change and grow up. As you get better, so will your environment. Ultimately, you'll get the outcome you want, a successful, productive and economically fruitful child. It's up to you, parents. Promote your education first, then promote your child's. Every parent has to get a high school diploma or GED first. When you get that high school diploma or GED, you empower yourself and you empower your community. And when you become a better person, you will get a better outcome, and that makes for better schools. These steps will lead to a decrease in conflicts between parents and teachers.

"Don't Kick Them Out!"
7 W's Of How To Manage Negative Student Behavior

7 W's Of How To Manage Negative Student Behavior

One major hurdle in our education and juvenile systems is managing negative behavior. For the last 30 years, negative behavior has become so dominant that it actually disrupts education. Our task is to help you understand what to do with negative behaviors that disrupt learning. We have to learn how to manage those negative behaviors effectively.

I am qualified to speak on this because I have been successful in treating some of the most violent juvenile offenders in America. I have had the people who commit the crimes that you read about under my care. Many are going to prison. Under my care, these violent young offenders have shown improvement in negative behavior. Over a three-year period, we've had one and a half fights and major cooperation in the treatment process. For a jail, that's unheard of. I understand how to aggressively attack and kill negative behaviors. I am skilled at fighting what is basically a form of terrorism, because negative behavior is an act of terrorism – it controls the environment, it has everybody on edge, it creates fear. When it comes to that negative behavior, you have to understand how to deal with it. The only way to beat a terrorist is to think like a terrorist.

My philosophy has always been that you can't kick them out. Now, we're not talking about kids who are violent or bring weapons to school. We have to think about that, because people who bring weapons to school need to be expelled. However, for the other cases, we have to figure out a way to effectively neutralize negative behavior, especially in urban, Title I schools. If we just kick them out, the demographics continue to fall. Districts can't handle the behavior, so half the population leaves the district and take these issues to charter schools. Fast forward 10 years, and public school districts are trying to attract students back because they went from a million kids to less than 200,000 in some big markets. That's a major financial problem.

When analyzing behavior for an effective result, you first have to figure out the seven Ws, **the first being what the behavior violation is**. I need to know what he/she did wrong so I know what we need to correct. Too many times, however, educators cannot convey what the behavior violation is. They say the child is angry, but that's not a behavior violation. He has a bad attitude. How is that a violation? You say it's more than one single action. I know what you're saying, but when you're trying to correct something, it has to be clarified. Where is the violation so we know what to correct. The student is quick to fight. That's deeper. He's easily influenced, withdrawn, disengaged. OK. Is it horseplay or attention deficit? Is it drug abuse? Is the person coming to school high and you're not addressing it? **What is the negative behavior conduct?** What is it that we need to correct?

Once we find out what the violation is, we need to find out the second W, **why the student is acting out**. What is the root cause of the behavior dysfunction? **It can always be traced back to the relationship, or lack of a relationship, with the father.** It wasn't the relationship the student wanted or needed. His love tank is not full and he is angry and hostile that his dad is not in his life the way they desire it. <u>**Needy, attention seeking behavior comes from being rejected by the one person you want and need love from the most.**</u> Plus, you have mothers who enable certain negative male behavior, saying, "Well, he does that sometimes." So what is the rule? Always go back to the daddy.

   Daddies dictate a child's emotional stability. When you see these behavior problems, you better know that you're dealing with a society that has a huge problem with daddy issues. This is the daddy issue generation. This is where the impact can be felt, because emotionally he's disconnected from us. These young people are feeling it, and they come to class seeking attention that they don't get in a normal situation. That's why they're disrupting your class. That's why they're talking out of turn. **We have to re-teach classroom etiquette.** We can no longer rely on these things being taught at home.

   As a teacher in the 21st century, you have to ask yourself what the relationship with that father is. Teachers who are really going to be successful have to break down those walls because the parent may not want to share what's going on. That can impede your progress.

   So we have what the behavior is and why it's happening. The next step is to determine the third W, <u>**when does the negative behavior shows itself**</u>. Is it more commonly seen in the morning?

After lunch? If we know when we can chart it. If we know when we find it happening, we can nip it in the bud.

Similar to knowing when the behavior happens, we need to find out the fourth W, **where is the environment when the child starts acting up**? Is it specific to one classroom? **This is important to watch out for because, for many students, their behavior is classroom specific.** They'll act one way in one teacher's room, then another way in another teacher's room.

This leads us to the fifth W, **what is it about you that makes the student act up in your classroom**? If a student exhibits a problem in one teacher's classroom but not another's, you need to determine why. I was at a school once with 10 teachers, and only two of those teachers didn't have problems. Why? They had better relationship with the students and management of their classroom. So you move that person out and put a new person in, i.e. a sub., and you see all kinds of behaviors popping up. **What is it about you that allows that?** What is it about you that makes a student conduct himself in this unhealthy, unproductive manner? This is un-reviewed data. We know the student has a problem, but what is it about us that perpetuates the problem?

Next, we need to ask ourselves the sixth W, **what are the consequences if we let this behavior go**? What will the consequences be to our life and to the student's life? I can give you clear factors. If you've got a high number of suspensions and expulsions, you are feeding the future of high incarceration. You are feeding your competition, the juvenile facility, which is taking students from public education and funding them at time and a half (meaning tuition and plus some). This is reality, and the consequence is that you have to say you produced an absolute loser.

We know the parent is the one who is supposed to coach kids and bring them to us ready to teach, but that is not happening. So what do we do? Complain? Then they blame us. There is no room for complaining in this competitive world education society. You need a solution. We need to evaluate and make adjustments. If we cannot manage it, we are just contributing to the world decapitation.

Finally, we need to find out the seventh W, **who or what is triggering the behavior**. Does the student see certain people? Does he see friends and act out? Does he see a teacher and act out? Does he see a girl and act out? What is the trigger: a claustrophobic person being in a small classroom? Having to sit still? Knowing what triggers this behavior, what triggers the fighting, the blurting out, the negative, disrespectful conduct to a teacher puts you in a place to understand the scope of the error so you can correct it.

Knowing the triggers also gives us a more comprehensive method of dealing with discipline onsite. The new model of discipline in all situations has to be handling discipline in the school. To do that, you need the right people, because not everybody manages discipline well. Many of us manage the classroom like we live our life, and a lot of us live our life very passive aggressive.

Teaching in urban areas, or with kids period in the 21st century, is not passive aggressive.

The other day, I was working with my daughter and her school. It was her first day of pre-K and they told me that she was crying and didn't want to write her name. Let me tell you something. I don't need a babysitter. I'm producing superstars. I'm training and raising CEOs. If she was crying, that teacher needed to tighten up and tell her to get up and write her name. Of course, you can say it the way you would say it, but the bottom line is you need to get her up. I'm not producing a loser, and I want the rigor in pushing kids to perform.

You've got to do it. The 21st century teacher takes on a coaching role, a person who pushes us forward and causes us to perform. That requires some spunk, and that is why you have some really good coaches who spur people toward high performance. They need to become the Tom Izzo's of the teaching world, pushing kids in the right direction. **This is the skill urban teachers in the 21st century have to learn.** There's no way around it. Teachers go from teaching to coaching. Many times, in urban Title I districts, that's what it is. Teachers teach them something, then coach them in it.

It's a new skill that teachers have to develop, and that's what we're here to do. We believe these things give you a framework to understand and identify some things that will put you in an ongoing position to identify and solve behavior problems. If you've got the right people, you have to clearly

Poor Kids Can Learn TOO!

communicate with them, and then create an environment in which these issues can be managed in your build or classroom. **Most behavior problems are environmentally specific.** <u>People don't act the same way everywhere</u>. That's fact. In our educational practices, our treatment practices, we have to understand there's something about the students/people; **1) communicating, and 2) the environment. This is facilitating and triggering and drawing the kind of behavior we don't want. <u>We need to adjust our attitudes and we have to understand that we can no longer rely on home training</u>.**

<u>As I always say, if you fix the people, you fix the problem.</u> This is how improve our process of in-school discipline management.

About The Author

Dr. Jesse W. Jackson III is a husband, father, consultant and licensed professional counselor who specializes in family and male college graduation success. Dr. Jackson holds master's and doctorate degrees in counseling from Wayne State University and Trinity Institute, respectively. Dr. Jackson has been in private practice since 1998. As a keynote speaker, seminar leader and licensed professional counselor, Dr. Jackson addresses more than 100,000 people each year.

Dr. Jackson has authored twenty books, five of which have become international bestsellers, including the male development classics; *The Best Man, College Or Prison: The Male Crisis Of The 21ˢᵗ Century, Black Males Can Graduate, $100,000: The New Minimal Wage, Divorce Is Not An Option, I'm Tired Of Being Broke,* and *Success Or Failure: Leaders Are The Difference.*

Dr. Jackson has served as a counselor, coach, and mentor on every K thru 12 level of education. He has also served on the faculty and staff of Wayne State University, Oakland Community College and North Dakota University as a guest instructor. Over his professional career he has extensively excelled in motivating African American youth toward attending post-secondary education while living drug & crime free lives.

Dr. Jackson has been instrumental in founding the Daddy Issues/Without A Father Syndrome diagnosis and treatment model. Dr. Jackson has embarked on a journey to help this fatherless generation to heal the emotional wounds from their failed or unfulfilled relationship with their father. Dr. Jackson teaches individuals how to identify the symptoms, and he walks his student through the spiritual and emotional detoxification healing process. Dr. Jackson exhaustive research on the effects of the father disconnection and absence on black children's confidence, emotional stability and ability to learn has respect been nationally respected and cited by his colleagues and students.

Dr. Jackson has continued to excel in helping school districts, organizations and colleges find effective solutions to improve black male graduation rates and black child academic and social achievement. Dr. Jackson is currently consulting with several universities to improve the male college completion rate.

Dr. Jackson travels extensively throughout the United States teaching and motivating elementary, junior high, high school, and college students and parents on the principles of college, career, and financial success.

To invite Dr. Jackson to speak at your school, business, organization, church or special event, contact him:
Jesse Jackson III
P.O. Box 80773 | Rochester, MI 48308
Website: www.jessejackson3rd.org
Email: info@jessejackson3rd.org
Phone: 1-888-987-5093 Fax: 888-215-6481

Poor Kids Can Learn TOO!

2013-2014 Professional Development Program
"Mastering Black Student Achievement"
(For K-12 & College Professionals)

Dr. Jesse W. Jackson III has established its reputation for excellence in the areas of black student success and professional development for the 21st century educator and human service professional. Dr. Jesse W. Jackson III's professional development program focuses on strengthening the core values of our schools with teamwork, professional ethics, professional values, diversity, instructional practices, and by promoting healthy lives for staff members. As society has presented my colleagues with more challenges, our company has specialized in providing the best solutions. This program consists of 7 sessions which includes:

1. Why Boys Hate School/ (Black Boys Can Learn): How to Teach and Engage Difficult Male Students in the Learning Process
2. How To Improve Teamwork and Build A Team Culture Amongst Professional Staff
3. "Who Is In Control?" The Pillars of 21st Century Classroom Management: How To Create A Powerful Learning Environment With Black Children
4. Don't Kick Them Out! How To Manage And Address Black Male Behavior Problems
5. Parents & Teachers Working Together: How To Decrease Black Parent and Staff Conflict
6. "The Welfare System In The Classroom", Increasing Diversity & Understanding of Poverty's Effect On Students
7. Poor Kids Can Learn TOO! How To Address Poverty & The Social And Emotional Learning Challenges Of Black Students

These are challenging sessions that address the worst problems in education today such as; male students lack of interest in school, discipline problems with males, conflicts between teachers and parents, male learning styles, and why the school system has been forever altered due to the demographic changes of today's students. These sessions will also help professional staff improve their quality of work performance and live more healthy lives.

All sessions includes materials for professional staff. **We will accommodate any financial arrangement that needs to be made for your school. We want you to maximize your dollars.**

All Schools Must Schedule A Minimum of Two Sessions
For more information concerning scheduling a seminar, seminar fees and packages, please feel free to contact me directly at 888-987-5093 or 248- 894-3912. I look forward to working with you soon.
Sincerely,

Dr. Jesse W. Jackson III
Student Success Consultant

Poor Kids Can Learn TOO!
98